D1302702

PRESENTED TO

Linda

FROM

Anne

DATE

5/18/05

Thank You

YOUR THOUGHTFULNESS IS APPRECIATED

DEBORAH BOONE AND CATHY HAKE

A DayMaker Greeting Book

Silent gratitude isn't
much use to anyone.

G. B. STERN

Thank you for...

YOUR ACT OF KINDNESS

YOUR THOUGHTFUL GIFT

BRIGHTENING MY DAY

YOUR WISE COUNSEL

BEING THERE WHEN
I NEEDED YOU

Thank You for...

YOUR ACT OF KINDNESS

Little deeds of kindness, little words of love,

help to make earth happy like the heaven above.

JULIA A. FLETCHER CARNEY

One can never pay in gratitude;

one can only pay "in kind" somewhere else in life. . . .

ANNE MORROW LINDBERGH

...For how many things,

which for our own sake

we never do,

do we perform

for the sake

of our friends.

MARCUS TULLIUS CICERO

Someday, I hope to
pass along the kindness
you have shown to me.

You know the value of silence.

Out of the abundance of your

heart you stepped in,

and your actions said more than

words ever could.

The glory of friendship is not in the outstretched hand, nor the kindly smile, nor the joy of companionship; it is in the spiritual inspiration that comes to one when he discovers that someone else believes in him and is willing to trust him.

RALPH WALDO EMERSON

The fruit of the Spirit is love, joy, peace, patience, kindness, goodness, faithfulness, gentleness and self-control.

GALATIANS 5:22–23

Saying is one thing, and doing is another.

MICHEL DE MONTAIGNE

Love has a hem to her garment

That reaches the very dust.

It sweeps the streets and lanes,

And because it can, it must.

MOTHER TERESA

She doeth little kindnesses which most
leave undone. . . .

JAMES RUSSELL LOWELL

A little word in kindness spoken,
A motion or a tear,
Has often healed the heart that's broken,
And made a friend sincere.

DANIEL CLEMENT COLESWORTHY

It is not so much our friends' help that
helps us, as the confidence of their help.

EPICURUS

I know I can

count on you.

You are always there

with open arms

and a willing heart.

You cannot do a kindness too soon

because you never know how soon it will be too late.

RALPH WALDO EMERSON

After the verb "to Love," "to Help" is

the most beautiful verb in the world.

BERTHA VON SUTTNER

At the most unexpected times,

a simple act can become profound. . . .

You helped me when I needed it most,

showing love in the most tangible way.

I'll never forget how you came alongside

and cared for me.

Thank You for...

YOUR THOUGHTFUL GIFT

Verily, great grace may go with a little gift;
And precious are all things that come from friends.

THEOCRITUS

"It is more blessed to give than to receive."

ACTS 20:35

My inclination is to say, "You shouldn't have," but knowing you as I do, you'll just shrug and act as if your gift was no big deal. Someone with a heart as big as yours deserves more than a simple thanks. So, I want to say...YOU BLESSED MY SOCKS OFF!

A friendship can weather most things and thrive
in thin soil; but it needs a little mulch of letters
and phone calls and small, silly presents every so
often—just to save it from drying out completely.

PAM BROWN

A generous man will prosper;
he who refreshes others will himself be refreshed.

PROVERBS 11:25

A thing of beauty is a joy forever;
Its loveliness increases.

JOHN KEATS

You know me so well...

...my favorite colors, music, and habits

...the tender things that touch my heart

...the bits of whimsy that make me laugh

The sensitivity and care you took in

choosing the right gift mean so much.

Blessed are those

who give

without remembering

and receive

without forgetting.

AUTHOR UNKNOWN

Good will come to him who is generous and lends freely,

who conducts his affairs with justice.

PSALM 112:5

Sometimes, in the busyness of daily life,

it's easy to overlook simple acts of generosity:

a borrowed cup of sugar,

a lent tool,

or extra minutes given freely.

When I saw this verse from the Psalms, I thought of you.

God is faithful to His promises. . . .

Surely He'll shower you with goodness and mercy.

Thank You for...

BRIGHTENING MY DAY

Kind words can be short and easy to speak,
but their echoes are truly endless.

MOTHER TERESA

Friends are the siblings God never gave us.

AUTHOR UNKNOWN

The real test of friendship is: Can you literally do
nothing with the other person? Can you enjoy together
those moments of life that are utterly simple? They are
the moments people look back on at the end of life and
number as their most sacred experiences.

EUGENE KENNEDY

We cannot really love anybody with
whom we never laugh.

AGNES REPPLIER

I appreciate the
treasure I find in you.

Trustworthy

Reassuring

Enthusiastic

Attentive ear

Sensitivity

Unwavering loyalty

Reliable

Enjoyable

Oh, the comfort, the inexpressible comfort

of feeling safe with a person;

having neither to weigh thoughts nor measure words,

but to pour them all out, just as they are,

chaff and grain together,

knowing that a faithful hand will take and sift them,

keep what is worth keeping,

and then, with a breath of kindness,

blow the rest away.

GEORGE ELIOT

There is divine purpose in bringing out the best
in one another.

DENIS WAITLEY

As iron sharpens iron,
so one man sharpens another.

PROVERBS 27:17

The greatest good you can do for one another
is not just to share your riches
but to reveal to him his own.

BENJAMIN DISRAELI

The capacity to care is the thing which gives
life its deepest meaning and significance.

PABLO CASALS

A friend may well be reckoned
the masterpiece of nature.

RALPH WALDO EMERSON

꧁

True friendship gives and takes—
a delicate balance based on
need. Lately it seems you've been
doing the most giving. I want you
to know I've noticed and cherish
all you've done for me.

There are days when it seems like my to-do list grows longer. More to do, less time in which to do it. Everything seems a little too hard, yet every task is so important. No spare moments to relax, to pick up a book, or even stop to smell a rose.

And then, you, my friend, come alongside. You arrive with a cheerful smile and roll up your sleeves—and two sets of hands begin working as one.

You refresh my spirit and lighten my load.

Thank you.

He is thy friend indeed,

He will help thee in thy need.

RICHARD BARNFIELD

The comfort of a friend is priceless.

You are one of God's sweetest gifts.

Thank You for...

YOUR WISE COUNSEL

Pleasant words are a honeycomb,

sweet to the soul and healing to the bones.

PROVERBS 16:24

Never take the advice of someone

who has not had your kind of trouble.

SIDNEY J. HARRIS

You alone understood. . . .

And the words you spoke were perfect.

The wise in heart are called discerning,

and pleasant words promote instruction.

PROVERBS 16:21

If you judge people, you have no time to love them.

MOTHER TERESA

When I needed counsel, you were there.

Thank you for your heartfelt words—

they meant the world to me!

A man finds joy in an apt reply—

and how good is a timely word!

PROVERBS 15:23

Perfume and incense bring joy to the heart,

and the pleasantness of one's friend

springs from his earnest counsel.

PROVERBS 27:9

Thank You for...

BEING THERE WHEN I NEEDED YOU

When we're at low ebb, sometimes just to see
the goodness radiating from another can be all
we need to rediscover it in ourselves.

KATHLEEN NORRIS

When it is dark enough, men can see stars.

RALPH WALDO EMERSON

God's promises are
like the stars;
the darker the night
the brighter they shine.

DAVID NICHOLAS

In the darkness of my life,

you stood beside me

and encouraged me to look up.

In the dark valley,

I knew I wasn't alone.

In your face,

I saw the reflection of God.

In your touch,

I felt His presence.

In your words,

I heard His voice.

Love seeketh not itself to please,

Nor for itself hath any care,

But for another gives it ease,

And builds a heaven in hell's despair.

WILLIAM BLAKE

Just to know someone cared. . . .

That was what I needed most.

In everyone's life, at some time, our inner fire goes out.
It is then burst into flame by an encounter with another
human being. We should all be thankful for those people
who rekindle the inner spirit.

ALBERT SCHWEITZER

When my world turned dark and bleak,

you held the torch of friendship.

In prosperity our friends know us;
in adversity we know our friends.

JOHN CHURTON COLLINS

Life is mostly froth and bubble,

Two things stand like stone,

KINDNESS in another's trouble,

COURAGE in your own.

ADAM LINDSAY GORDON

It's so hard to find the right words to say. The help you gave and the strength you lent made all of the difference.

Thank you for listening to the still voice of God, for obeying it, and for ministering to me as you did.

A friend loves at all times.

PROVERBS 17:17

Holding the heart of another in the
comforting hands of prayer is a
priceless act of love.

JANET L. WEAVER

Friendship redoubleth joys

and cutteth grief in half.

FRANCIS BACON

———————————

Two are better than one. . . .

If one falls down,

his friend can help him up.

ECCLESIASTES 4:9–10

———————————

No one is useless in this world

who lightens the burdens of another.

CHARLES DICKENS

God does notice us, and He watches over us.
But it is usually through another person
that He meets our needs.

SPENCER W. KIMBALL

You were there, by God's design,

at exactly the right moment.

Thank you.

Dear friend,

You've been there for me so many times—
whether with a sweet or silly gift,
a comforting hug, helping hands, or a listening ear.
You always seem to know what I need most.
There aren't words enough to say how I appreciate you.
Your thoughtfulness makes such a difference.

God bless you!

© 2003 by Barbour Publishing, Inc.

ISBN 1-58660-931-9

Design by Lookout Design Group, Inc.

All rights reserved. No part of this publication may be reproduced or transmitted in any form or by any means without written permission of the publisher.

All Scripture quotations are taken from the HOLY BIBLE, NEW INTERNATIONAL VERSION®. NIV®. Copyright © 1973, 1978, 1984 by International Bible Society. Used by permission of Zondervan Publishing House. All rights reserved.

Published by Barbour Publishing, Inc., P.O. Box 719, Uhrichsville, Ohio 44683, www.barbourbooks.com

Printed in China.
5 4 3 2 1